Bond
No.1 for exam success

English
10 Minute Tests
8–9 years

OXFORD
UNIVERSITY PRESS

TEST 1: **Mixed**

Test time: 0 — 5 — 10 minutes

Add the *suffix* able or ible to each of these to make a word.

1 excit_____

2 divis_____

3 agree_____

4 forgiv_____

5 revers_____

6 avoid_____

Change the underlined words into a *pronoun*.

7 The new puppy is <u>my puppy</u>.

The new puppy is _____.

8 The red sports car is <u>the Frost family's</u>.

The red sports car is _____.

9 Her house is next to <u>our house</u>.

Her house is next to _____.

10 The coat on the ground is <u>Jacob's</u>.

The coat on the ground is _____.

Write an *antonym* for each word.

11 scream _____

12 stand _____

13 build _____

14 smile _____

15 quiet _____

16 outside _____

Copy these sentences and add the missing punctuation.

17 Have you fed the dog this morning asked Dad

_____

_____

18 Mum moaned Time I mowed the lawn again

_____

_____

19 Can we go swimming this afternoon Alex and Tom pleaded

_____

_____

20 Poppy said I can't wait until your birthday party

_____

_____

TEST 2: **Spelling**

Test time: 0 — 5 — 10 minutes

Add gue or que to complete these words.

1 lea _____

2 uni _____

3 anti _____

4 ton _____

Circle the silent letter in each of these words.

5 fascinate

6 crescent

7 scent

8 discipline

9 scissors

10 science

Add the missing double letters to each of these words.

11 fla __ __ el

12 spa __ __ ow

13 ye __ __ ow

14 ke __ __ le

15 sa __ __ le

16 wri __ __ le

17 po __ __ ute

18 le __ __ on

Spell each of these words correctly. Some need a letter added, some need a letter changed.

19 sceme

20 mashine

21 caracter

22 broshure

23 shef

24 eco

25 corus

4

Total

TEST 3: **Spelling**

Test time: 0 — 5 — 10 minutes

Write a *homophone* for each of these words.

1 knew _____
2 seen _____
3 bored _____
4 sighed _____
5 source _____
6 dear _____
7 piece _____

Write each of these *nouns* in their *plural* form.

8 church _____
9 valley _____
10 knife _____
11 baby _____
12 clock _____
13 café _____
14 kilo _____
15 dish _____

Circle the correct spelling of each word.

16 height   hieght
17 aweful   awful
18 favourite   favorite
19 quater   quarter
20 naghty   naughty
21 adress   address
22 famous   famos
23 various   varius
24 library   libary
25 roze   rose

5

Total

TEST 4: Comprehension

Read this extract carefully.

The Best Birthday Present

by Ruud van der Rol and Rian Verhoeven

1 Anne Frank woke early at six o'clock in the morning on Friday, 12th June. She could hardly wait to get out of bed. That she was up so early was not surprising, since today
5 was her thirteenth birthday.

It was wartime, 1942. Anne was living with her father and mother and her sister, Margot, who was three years older than Anne, in a housing development
10 in Amsterdam, the capital city of the Netherlands. The Netherlands had been occupied for two years by the Germans, who had launched a campaign of discrimination and persecution against the
15 Jews. It was becoming increasingly difficult for Jews such as the Frank family to lead ordinary lives, but Anne was not thinking about that on her birthday.

At seven o'clock she went to her parents'
20 bedroom. Then the whole family gathered together in the living room to unwrap Anne's presents.

Anne received many gifts that day, including books, a jigsaw puzzle, a
25 brooch, and candy. But her best present was one given by her parents that morning: a hardcover diary, bound in red and white checkered cloth. She had never had a diary before and was delighted
30 with the gift. Anne had many friends, both boys and girls, but with them she talked only about everyday things. But now Anne's diary would be her very best friend, a friend she could trust with
35 everything. She called her new friend "Kitty".

I hope I shall be able to confide in you completely, as I have never been able to do in anyone before, and I hope that you will be a
40 *great support and comfort to me.* Anne Frank (12 June 1942)

On the inside of the cover she stuck a photograph of herself, and wrote next to it: *Gorgeous photo, isn't it!!!*

45 Anne started writing to Kitty in her diary two days later, on Sunday, June 14. She would continue filling it for just over two years with her thoughts and feelings, and stories about all the things
50 that happened to her. But on that first day, she could not suspect how her life was suddenly to change completely. Nor could she imagine that later millions of people throughout the world would read
55 her diary.

Anne and her family went into hiding on 6 July 1942 in fear that if they didn't, the Germans would arrest and possibly kill them. They stayed in hiding for more than two years until they were finally betrayed. When the Franks were taken away by the Germans, Anne's diary was left behind. Only Anne's father survived the war and he had her diary published in 1947.

Answer these questions about the extract.

1 Why was 12th June an important day for Anne?

2 Where did Anne live?

3 How much older than Anne was her sister?

4 What was Anne's 'best present'?

5 Why do you think Anne was so delighted with this present?

6 For how long did Anne write to 'Kitty'?

7 What is meant by 'The Netherlands had been occupied for two years by the Germans' (lines 11–12)?

8 Anne's diary is now very famous and read by millions of people. How do you think Anne would have felt about this?

Time for a break! Go to Puzzle Page 38

TEST 5: **Vocabulary**

Test time: 0 — 5 — 10 minutes

Write these words in *alphabetical order*.

garlic   garden   gangster   garage   gateau

1 (1) _____

2 (2) _____

3 (3) _____

4 (4) _____

5 (5) _____

Write a *definition* for each of these words.

6 school

_____

7 tube

_____

8 rabbit

_____

9 adult

_____

10 hour

_____

8

Draw a line to match a word in the first column with a word in the second column to make a *compound word*.

11–15
any   head

card   room

red   where

water   board

class   fall

Write a *synonym* for each word.

16 active _____

17 angry _____

18 run _____

19 repair _____

20 hate _____

9

Total

Test 6: Mixed

Add the missing apostrophes to each sentence.

1 Lets have a race!

2 Ill remember to bring my book.

3 Theres another way to get to the park.

4 What shall I say weve been doing?

5 I cant believe we are lost again!

Write these sentences in their *plural* form.

Example: The person walked into the shop. *The people walked into the shops.*

6 The dog chased the ball.

_____

7 School is closed on Tuesday.

_____

8 The Sun shone and made the flower grow.

_____

9 The car sped down the country lane.

_____

Circle the masculine words.

10–14   prince   duchess   queen

   gander   duke   nephew

   madam   waiter   niece

Add the missing 'y' to each of these words.

15   rhme   _____

16   mstery   _____

17   gm   _____

18   phsical   _____

19   mth   _____

20   encclopedia _____

TEST 7: Grammar

Underline the *verb* in each line.

1	he	dog	flap	sadly	hive
2	kite	hill	scream	they	brown
3	when	growl	bucket	lovely	sister
4	scratch	biro	on	bungalow	you

Write an interesting *adjective* to describe each of these *nouns*.

5 a _____ gate

6 a _____ house

7 a _____ lamb

8 a _____ bike

9 a _____ T-shirt

Write two examples of an *adverb*.

10–11 _____   _____

Rewrite the *proper nouns* with capital letters.

mobile phone   chicken   roald dahl

jupiter   homework   biscuit

tower of london   computer   banana

12 _____

13 _____

14 _____

Write one of the following *conjunctions* in each gap so that every sentence makes sense. Each word may be used only once.

because   and   after   so   but   while

15 Hannah held Ben's bike _____ he went into the shop.

16 Veejay had his tea _____ finishing his homework.

17 Aimee enjoys going to Dancing Club _____ loves Gym Club more.

18 Dan ran home from school _____ he wanted to watch something on television.

19 A loudspeaker was used by Mrs Golding _____ all the children could hear clearly.

20 Dad made the sandwiches _____ then put them in the rucksack.

Test 8: Comprehension

Read this extract carefully.

The Butterfly Lion *by Michael Morpurgo*

1   *Bertie was born in South Africa, in a remote farmhouse near a place called Timbavati.*

One evening – Bertie must have been six years old by now – he was sitting high up
5   in the branches of a tree, hoping against hope the lions might come down for their sunset drink as they often did. He was thinking of giving up, for it would soon be too dark to see much now, when he
10 saw a solitary lioness come down to the waterhole. Then he saw that she was not alone. Behind her, and on unsteady legs, came what looked like a lion cub – but it was white, glowing white in the gathering
15 gloom of dusk.

While the lioness drank, the cub played at catching her tail; and then, when she had had her fill, the two of them slipped away into the long grass and were gone.

20 Bertie ran inside, screaming with excitement. He had to tell someone, anyone. He found his father working at his desk.

"Impossible," said his father. "You're
25 seeing things that aren't there, or you're telling fibs – one of the two."

"I saw him. I promise," Bertie insisted.

But his father would have none of it, and sent him to his room for arguing.

30 His mother came to see him later.

"Anyone can make a mistake, Bertie dear," she said. "It must have been the sunset. It plays tricks with your eyes sometimes. There's no such thing as a
35 white lion."

The next evening Bertie watched again at the fence, but the white lion cub and the lioness did not come, nor did they the next evening, nor the next.

40 Bertie began to think he must have been dreaming it.

A week or more passed, and there had been only a few zebras and wildebeest down at the waterhole. Bertie was already
45 upstairs in his bed when he heard his father riding into the compound, and then the stamp of his heavy boots on the veranda.

"We got her! We got her!" he was
50 saying. "Huge lioness, massive she was. She's taken half a dozen of my best cattle in the last two weeks. Well, she won't be taking any more."

Bertie's heart stopped. In that one
55 terrible moment he knew which lioness his father was talking about. There could be no doubt in it. His white lion cub had been orphaned.

Answer these questions about the extract.

1. In which country was Bertie born?
   _____

2. Where was Bertie sitting while waiting for the lions?
   _____

3. What was so special about the lion cub Bertie spotted that evening?
   _____

4. Why did Bertie's dad send Bertie to his room?
   _____
   _____
   _____

5. What other animals does Bertie see at the waterhole?
   _____

6. Why did Bertie begin to doubt what he'd seen?
   _____
   _____

7. Which line in the extract tells how Bertie felt on hearing the news the lioness had been killed?
   _____

8. What do you think Bertie does next?
   _____
   _____

Time for a break! Go to Puzzle Page 39

Test 9: **Mixed**

Test time: 0 – 5 – 10 minutes

Rewrite this short passage, adding the missing capital letters.

1–6 najib called to his friend, "quick, if we don't hurry we will miss the party!" henry wasn't sure he wanted to go all the way to stafford but he grabbed his jumper anyway. "coming, i'm coming," he moaned.

Add its or it's to each gap in the sentences.

7 _____ a very sunny day.

8 Look at the baby bird on the ground. How will it find _____ nest?

9 The puppy has chewed my slippers again. _____ getting beyond a joke!

10 The school has _____ playground at the back of the building.

Circle the *collective nouns*.

11–13 mouse   gate   Portsmouth

bouquet   Hannah   tribe

lantern   glass   box

flock   poodle   building

Add ory, ary or ery to make a word.

14 deliv_____

15 prim_____

16 machin_____

17 mem_____

18 Janu_____

19 laborat_____

20 discov_____

Test 10: Spelling

Add the *prefix* re, un, non or dis to each of these words.

1 _____sense
2 _____call
3 _____fair
4 _____aware
5 _____honest
6 _____continue
7 _____visit
8 _____ability

Put a tick next to the words spelt correctly and a cross next to those spelt incorrectly.

9 weigh _____
10 thuoght _____
11 vien _____
12 double _____
13 tuch _____
14 nieghbour _____
15 country _____
16 truble _____
17 yuong _____
18 they _____

Add the *suffix* to each word. Don't forget any necessary spelling changes.

19 expand + sion _____
20 simple + ly _____
21 magic + ian _____
22 angry + ly _____
23 confuse + sion _____
24 prepare + tion _____
25 televise + sion _____

TEST 11: **Spelling**

Test time: 0 — 5 — 10 minutes

> Add the *suffix* ous to these root words. Watch out, some of the root words need to change.

1. poison _____
2. outrage _____
3. mountain _____
4. joy _____
5. peril _____

6. vigour _____
7. danger _____
8. nerve _____
9. humour _____
10. courage _____

> Add the *suffix* tion or sion to make a word.

11. frac_____
12. inva_____
13. direc_____
14. deci_____

15. men_____
16. occa_____
17. televi_____
18. subtrac_____

> Add ie or ei to each of these to make a word.

19. th __ __ f
20. p __ __ ce
21. f __ __ ld
22. w __ __ gh

23. __ __ ght
24. v __ __ n
25. c __ __ ling

19

Total

Test 12: Sentences

Add the missing punctuation to the end of each sentence.

1. Why haven't I been given a present ___
2. The team waited in line to board the coach ___
3. Watch out, that car is heading for you ___
4. Do you want to borrow my bike ___
5. I think I'm stuck, help ___
6. Mum put the glass of water on the table ___

Copy these sentences, adding the missing speech marks'.

7. Tania whispered, Quiet or we will wake Grandad.

8. Where is the best place to fish? Tom asked Yousef.

9. Helen giggled, Why are you wearing that strange-looking hat?

10. I love you, said Seamus as he cuddled his puppy.

Make a *noun phrase* for each of these nouns and add it to a sentence.

11 spider

_____

_____

12 baby

_____

_____

13 car

_____

_____

14 shadow

_____

_____

Add the missing apostrophes in these *phrases*.

15 the two horses reins

16 the four boys hats

17 the five pupils books

18 the Prime Ministers socks

19 the twelve cars wheels

20 the old mans shoes

Time for a break! Go to Puzzle Page 40

TEST 13: Comprehension

Read this poem carefully.

Leisure Centre, Pleasure Centre *by John Rice*

1 You go through plate glass doors
with giant red handles,
into light that's as bright
as a million candles.
5 The chlorine smells
the whole place is steaming,
the kids are yelling
and the kids are screaming.

Watch them
10 wave jump
dive thump
cartwheel
free wheel
look cute
15 slip chute
toe stub
nose rub
in the leisure centre, pleasure centre.

Sporty people laugh and giggle
20 folk in swimsuits give a wiggle.
Kids are in the café busy thinking
if they can afford some fizzy drinking.
In the changing rooms
wet folk shiver.
25 It's hard to get dressed
when you shake and quiver.

And we go
breast stroke
back stroke
30 two stroke

big folk
hair soak
little folk
eye poke
35 no joke
in the leisure centre, pleasure centre.

And now we are driving back home
fish 'n' chips in the car,
eyes are slowly closing
40 but it's not very far.
Snuggle wuggle up in fresh clean sheets
a leisure centre trip
is the best of treats because you can
keep fit
45 leap sit
eat crisps
do twists
belly flop
pit stop
50 fill up
with 7-Up
get going
blood flowing
look snappy
55 be happy
in the leisure centre, pleasure centre.

Test 1: Mixed (pages 2–3)

1–6 As a general rule (although there are exceptions), if the root word looks like a whole word, the suffix will most likely be '-able'; if the root word does not look like a whole word, the suffix will most likely be '-ible'.
1 **able** excitable The root word is excite (the 'e' is removed when adding the suffix).
2 **ible** divisible
3 **able** agreeable The root word is agree.
4 **able** forgivable The root word is forgive (the 'e' is removed when adding the suffix).
5 **ible** reversible The root word is reverse, so this is an exception to the rule.
6 **able** avoidable The root word is avoid.

7–10 Refer to definition of pronoun in key words on page 43.
7 **mine**
8 **theirs**
9 **ours**
10 **his**

11–16 Refer to definition of antonym in key words on page 43. Possible answers include:
11 *whisper*
12 *move*
13 *destroy*
14 *frown*
15 *noise*
16 *inside*

17–20 Speech is surrounded by speech marks (also known as inverted commas). There must be punctuation before the clause introducing the speech if the speech isn't at the start of the sentence (e.g. Q18 and Q20). There must also be punctuation before the closing speech mark.
17 "Have you fed the dog this morning?" asked Dad.
18 Mum moaned, "Time I mowed the lawn again."
19 "Can we go swimming this afternoon?" Alex and Tom pleaded.
20 Poppy said, "I can't wait until your birthday party."

Test 2: Spelling (page 4)

1 **gue** league
2 **que** unique
3 **que** antique
4 **gue** tongue

5–10 The letters 'sc' can represent a s sound; in this case, the 'c' is commonly referred to as a silent letter.
5 fas**c**inate
6 cres**c**ent
7 s**c**ent
8 dis**c**ipline
9 s**c**issors
10 s**c**ience

11 **flannel**
12 **sparrow**
13 **yellow**
14 **kettle**
15 **saddle**
16 **wriggle**
17 **pollute**
18 **lesson**

19 s**ch**eme The letters 'ch' can represent a k sound; in this case, the letter 'h' is commonly referred to as a silent letter.
20 ma**ch**ine The letters 'ch' can also represent a sh sound.
21 **ch**aracter Refer to Q19.
22 bro**ch**ure Refer to Q20.
23 **ch**ef Refer to Q20.
24 e**ch**o Refer to Q19.
25 **ch**orus Refer to Q19.

Test 3: Spelling (page 5)

1–7 Refer to definition of homophone in key words on page 43.
1 **new**
2 **scene**
3 **board**
4 **side**
5 **sauce**
6 **deer**
7 **peace**

8–15 Refer to definition of noun and plural in key words on page 43.
8 **churches** Words ending in 's', 'sh', 'ch', 'x', or 'z' can be made plural by adding 'es'.
9 **valleys** Most singular words can be made plural by adding an 's'.
10 **knives** Words ending in 'f' or 'fe' can be made plural by changing the 'f' or 'fe' to 'ves'.
11 **babies** Words ending in 'y' can be made plural by changing the 'y' to 'ies'.
12 **clocks** Refer to Q9.
13 **cafés** Refer to Q9.
14 **kilos** Refer to Q9.
15 **dishes** Refer to Q8.
16 **height**
17 **awful**
18 **favourite**
19 **quarter**

20 naughty
21 address
22 famous
23 various
24 library
25 rose

Test 4: Comprehension (pages 6–7)

1 **It was her birthday.** (line 5)
2 **Amsterdam** (line 10)
3 **three years** (lines 8–9)
4 **a diary** (lines 25–27)
5 *Anne was delighted with this present as, for her, the diary was a new friend with whom she could trust everything.*
6 **more than two years** (lines 47–48)
7 *The Netherlands had been under the control of the Germans for two years OR Germany had conquered the Netherlands two years earlier.*
8 *Anne might have been excited and touched that so many people were interested in her life and what she'd written.*

Test 5: Vocabulary (pages 8–9)

1–5 Refer to definition of alphabetical order in key words on page 43.
1 **gangster**
2 **garage**
3 **garden**
4 **garlic**
5 **gateau**
6–10 Refer to definition of definition in key words on page 43. Possible answers include:
6 *a place where people learn*
7 *a hollow pipe*
8 *a furry animal with long ears*
9 *a fully grown man, woman or animal*
10 *a unit of time, 60 minutes*
11–15 Refer to definition of compound word in key words on page 43.
anywhere, cardboard, redhead, waterfall, classroom
16–20 Refer to definition of synonym in key words on page 43. Possible answers include:
16 *busy*
17 *mad*
18 *sprint*
19 *mend*
20 *dislike*

Test 6: Mixed (pages 10–11)

1–5 Apostrophes are used for contractions (also known as for omission) when two words are combined and a letter is omitted, e.g. 'do not' becomes 'don't', with the apostrophe indicating the missing 'o'.
1 **Let's** Let + us ('u' is omitted)
2 **I'll** I + will ('wi' is omitted)
3 **There's** There + is ('i' is omitted)
4 **we've** we + have ('ha' is omitted)
5 **can't** can + not ('no' is omitted)
6–9 Refer to definition of plural in key words on page 43. Refer to Test 3 Q9.
6 The dogs chased the balls.
7 Schools are closed on Tuesdays.
8 The Sun shone and made the flowers grow.
9 The cars sped down the country lanes.
10–14 **prince, gander, duke, nephew, waiter**
15–20 The letter 'y' can represent the long i vowel sound, as in 'cry', or the short i vowel sound, as in 'big'.
15 **rhyme**
16 **mystery**
17 **gym**
18 **physical**
19 **myth**
20 **encyclopedia**

Test 7: Grammar (pages 12–13)

1–4 Refer to definition of verb in key words on page 43.
1 **flap**
2 **scream**
3 **growl**
4 **scratch**
5–9 Refer to definition of adjective in key words on page 43. Possible answers include:
5 *squeaky*
6 *haunted*
7 *bouncy*
8 *muddy*
9 *torn*
10–11 Refer to definition of adverb in key words on page 43. Possible answers include:
10–11 *calmly, quickly*
12–14 Refer to definition of proper noun in key words on page 43.
Roald Dahl, Jupiter, Tower of London
15–20 Refer to definition of conjunction in key words on page 43.

15 while
16 after
17 but
18 because
19 so
20 and

Test 8: Comprehension (pages 14–15)

1 **South Africa** (line 1)
2 **high in the branches of a tree** (lines 4–5)
3 **It was white.** (line 14)
4 *He felt there was no such thing as a white lion cub but Bertie kept arguing that there was.* (lines 24–29)
5 **zebras and wildebeest** (line 43)
6 *Day after day he waited for the lion cub and it didn't return.* (lines 36–39)
7 **Line 54** 'Bertie's heart stopped.'
8 *He might go out on his own searching for the white lion cub.*

Test 9: Mixed (pages 16–17)

1–6 Capital letters should be used for proper nouns (refer to definition of proper noun in key words on page 43) or at the start of a sentence.
1–6 Najib called to his friend, "Quick, if we don't hurry we will miss the party!" Henry wasn't sure he wanted to go all the way to Stafford but he grabbed his jumper anyway. "Coming, I'm coming," he moaned.
7–10 'Its' is a possessive determiner showing when something belongs to 'it'. 'It's' is a contraction of 'it is'.
7 **It's**
8 **its**
9 **It's**
10 **its**
11–13 Refer to definition of collective noun in key words on page 43.
bouquet, tribe, flock
14 **ery** delivery
15 **ary** primary
16 **ery** machinery
17 **ory** memory
18 **ary** January
19 **ory** laboratory
20 **ery** discovery

Test 10: Spelling (page 18)

1–8 Refer to definition of prefix in key words on page 43.
1 **nonsense**
2 **recall**
3 **unfair**
4 **unaware**
5 **dishonest**
6 **discontinue**
7 **revisit**
8 **disability**
9–18 The letters 'ei' and 'ey' can both represent an ay sound, as in 'beige' or 'grey'. The letters 'ou' can represent an uh sound, as in 'rough'.
9 ✓
10 ⚡
11 ⚡
12 ✓
13 ⚡
14 ⚡
15 ✓
16 ⚡
17 ⚡
18 ✓
19–25 Refer to definition of suffix in key words on page 43.
19 **expansion** When adding the suffix 'sion' to words ending in 'd', the 'd' is removed.
20 **simply** When adding the suffix 'ly' to words ending in 'le', the 'le' is removed.
21 **magician**
22 **angrily** When adding suffixes to words ending in 'y' with a consonant before it, the 'y' changes to 'i', but only if the root word has more than one syllable.
23 **confusion** When adding suffixes to words ending in 'se', the 'se' is removed.
24 **preparation** When adding the suffix 'tion' to words ending in 'ne', 've' or 're', change the final 'e' to 'a'.
25 **television** Refer to Q23.

Test 11: Spelling (page 19)

1–18 Refer to definition of suffix in key words on page 43.
1–10 Most often, the usual rules apply for adding suffixes beginning with vowel letters – there is no change to the root word. If the root word ends in an 'e', it is usually removed before adding the suffix.
1 **poisonous**
2 **outrageous** This is an exception to the rule.

3 **mountainous**
4 **joyous**
5 **perilous**
6 **vigorous** This is an exception to the rule.
7 **dangerous**
8 **nervous**
9 **humorous** This is an exception to the rule.
10 **courageous** This is an exception to the rule.
11–18 'sion' is used if the root words ends in 'se', 'd' or 'de'; 'tion' is used if the root word ends in 't' or 'te'.
11 **fraction**
12 **invitation** The root word is invite.
13 **direction** The root word is direct.
14 **decision** The root word is decide.
15 **mention**
16 **occasion**
17 **television** The root word is televise.
18 **subtraction** The root word is subtract.
19–25 When the sound is ee, use 'ie' (e.g. belief); when the sound is ay, use 'ei' (e.g. neighbour).
19 **thief**
20 **piece**
21 **field**
22 **weigh**
23 **eight**
24 **vein**
25 **ceiling** The sound is ee, but the rule 'i' before 'e' except after 'c' applies here.

Test 12: Sentences (pages 20–21)

1 ?
2 .
3 !
4 ?
5 !
6 .
7–10 Refer to Test 1 Q17–20.
7 Tania whispered, "Quiet or we will wake Grandad."
8 "Where is the best place to fish?" Tom asked Yousef.
9 Helen giggled, "Why are you wearing that strange-looking hat?"
10 "I love you," said Seamus as he cuddled his puppy.
11–14 Refer to definition of noun phrase in key words on page 43. Possible answers include:
11 *The terrified spider froze as the bird flew by.*
12 *The cuddly baby giggled as its grandmother gave it a hug.*
13 *Tim stopped to watch as a fast red car sped down the lane.*
14 *Sarah ran from the monster, trying to hide in the dark, cold shadow of the castle wall.*
15–20 Refer to definition of phrase in key words on page 43. Apostrophes used to indicate possession come after the noun and are followed by the letter 's'. Apostrophes used to mark <u>plural</u> possession come after the plural noun, which often ends in 's'; in this case, the extra 's' that usually follows the apostrophe is not needed.
15 **the two horses' reins**
16 **the four boys' hats**
17 **the five pupils' books**
18 **the Prime Minister's socks**
19 **the twelve cars' wheels**
20 **the old man's shoes**

Test 13: Comprehension (pages 22–23)

1 **a visit to a leisure centre with a swimming pool**
2 Answers could include any three of: *the bright lights, the chlorine smell, the warmth from the steam, the noise from the children.*
3 **cute** (line 14)
4 **whether they can afford a fizzy drink** (line 22)
5 *You shake and quiver when you are cold and wet.* (lines 25–26)
6 *how tired the visitors are on their way home*
7 Answers could include any three of: *toe stub, eye poke, being cold after swimming, noisy crowds*
8 *because it is about how much pleasure the leisure centre gives to visitors*

Test 14: Mixed (pages 24–25)

1 **thorough – borough**
2 **rough – tough**
3 **nought – thought**
4 **though – dough**
5 **plough – bough**
6–10 Refer to definition of definition in key words on page 43. Possible answers include:
6 *a book that gives the meaning of words*
7 *a book containing a daily record of personal experiences or observations*
8 *commonplace, usual*
9 *the second month in the year*
10 *the edge of an area*
11–15 Refer to definition of conjunction in key words on page 43.
11 At last Dad arrived home **so** we could eat our tea.
12 The wind rustled in the trees **as** darkness fell.
13 Jemma concentrated hard on her game of chess **because** it was an important match.
14 Daxa picked up the bags **and** carried them into the house.

15 The phone rang **but** nobody was home.
16–20 Commas are used to separate items in a list. There is a comma between each item except for the final two, which are separated by 'and' instead. Commas are also used to separate the main clause in a sentence from the added information.
16 Lia packed her hairbrush, nightie and toothbrush.
17 Despite the tent being hot and stuffy, Abi found it fairly comfortable.
18–19 When Daniel returned from school, he did his homework, practised the piano, walked the dog and cleaned the fish tank. (The comma after 'school' is optional.)
20 Sarah ran down the lane, her school bag bumping against her leg.

Test 15: Vocabulary (pages 26–27)

1–5 Refer to definition of antonym in key words on page 43. Possible answers include:
1 *finish*
2 *pull*
3 *sad*
4 *punishment*
5 *stiff*
6–10 Refer to definition of alphabetical order in key words on page 43.
6 **tarantula**
7 **target**
8 **tarnish**
9 **tart**
10 **tartan**
11–13 Refer to definition of diminutive in key words on page 43.
11 **duckling**
12 **piglet**
13 **gosling**
14–15 Refer to definition of homonym in key words on page 43. Possible answers include:
14 *My grandfather used to work in a coal mine.*
15 *That football is mine, not yours.*
16 **dress – frock**
17 **glasses – spectacles**
18 **schoolbag – satchel**
19 **radio – wireless**
20 **jug – pitcher**

Test 16: Mixed (pages 28–29)

1–5 Refer to definitions of plural and singular in key words on page 43. Refer to Test 3 Q8–11.
1 **engine**
2 **fox**
3 **fly**
4 **scarf**
5 **drum**
6–9 Refer to definition of adjectival phrase in key words on page 43. Possible answers include:
6 *loud, black*
7 *cold, heavy*
8 *young, jumping*
9 *sweet, juicy*
10–15 To decide whether to use 'sure' or 'ture', say the word out loud. Words with a sh sound in the middle are spelled 'sure'. Words with a tch sound in the middle are spelled 'ture'.
10 **sure** exposure
11 **ture** mature
12 **ture** signature
13 **sure** displeasure
14 **ture** miniature
15 **sure** pressure
16–20 Refer to Test 12 Q15–20.
16 **Kate's homework**
17 **my country's flag**
18 **Liam's computer**
19 **Meena's cakes**
20 **the birds' nests**

Test 17: Grammar (pages 30–31)

1–4 Refer to definition of adverb in key words on page 43.
1 **noisily**
2 **awkwardly**
3 **sleepily**
4 **hastily**
5–10 Refer to definitions of adjective and pronoun in key words on page 43. Possible answers include:
5–10 Three different sentences, e.g. *Paul said that he was cold. Soraya claimed the yellow sunhat was hers. They raced towards the rusty gates.*
11–14 Refer to definition of verb in key words on page 43. Possible answers include:
11 *gulp*
12 *grab*
13 *sniff*
14 *chat*
15–20 Refer to definitions of noun, common noun, proper noun and collective noun in key words on page 43.
15–20

Common nouns	Proper nouns	Collective nouns
kite	Wednesday	batch
mosquito	Buckingham Palace	bunch

Test 18: Comprehension (pages 32–33)

1 **huge balls of searing hot gas** (line 3)
2 **because they lie many million kilometres away** (lines 4–5)
3 **the Sun** (lines 10–12)
4 **a dwarf star** (lines 17–18)
5–6 *Stars twinkle because the light they shine bends. Some of the light bends and we can see it but some of it bends away from Earth and we can't see it. This makes it look like the stars are twinkling.*
7 *a star that has swelled up, before it changes into a black dwarf or explodes* (lines 36–40)
8 Child's own questions, e.g. *How hot are stars? Why do some stars explode?*

Test 19: Mixed (pages 34–35)

1 "**Where is your hat?**" called Dad.
2 Angus screamed, "**Watch out!**"
3 "**Let's go to the beach**," suggested Maria.
4 "**I can't wait until my birthday**," said Joe.
5 ✗
6 ✓
7 ✓
8 ✓
9 ✗
10 ✗
11–14 Refer to definition of verb in key words on page 43.
11 I **did** my homework correctly.
12 We **were** late for the party.
13 We **did** an excellent presentation.
14 I **was** tired after swimming.
15–20 Refer to definition of root word in key words on page 43.
15 **end**less The suffix -less has been added.
16 **print**er The suffix -er has been added.
17 **bi**cycle The prefix bi- has been added.
18 **trick**ery The suffix -ery has been added.
19 **collect**or The suffix -or has been added.
20 **un**clean The prefix un- has been added.

Test 20: Sentences (pages 36–37)

1–4 Refer to Test 14 Q16–20.
1 Riding on the tractor, Kyle felt like a farmer, just like his uncle. (The comma after 'tractor' is optional.)
2 The puppies chewed shoes, furniture and their beds!
3 The ponies jumped the fence, cantering up the lane towards the busy road.
4 Meena's sandwiches were filled with cheese**,** ham and mayonnaise.
5–9 Refer to definition of contraction in key words on page 43.
5 can't
6 could've
7 I'll
8 isn't
9 haven't
10–17 Refer to Test 9 Q1–6.
10–17 Chris rushed out of the front door and headed down Thresher Lane. He was late for football again. Ken, the coach, had threatened to throw him off the team if he didn't show for practice. Why was it that his mum, Liz, always arrived home late on a Tuesday?
18–20 Refer to definition of *fronted adverbial* in key words on page 43. Possible answers include:
18–20 *Every Friday, I have netball practice. On the horizon, storm clouds were gathering. Gradually, the stray dog began to trust me.*

Puzzle 1 (page 38)

TROUGH PLOUGH
NOUGHT COUGH
DOUGH   DROUGHT
SOUGHT THOUGHT

Puzzle 2 (page 39)

narrow, signal, lovely, though, circle, school, fright, lesson, charge, belief, window

Puzzle 3 (page 40)

duet – a song sung by two people
tricycle – a three-wheeled bike
decade – a ten-year period
double – two of the same thing
century – a hundred years
quartet – a group of four musicians
duel – a fight between two people
triplets – three babies born at a similar time to the same mother

Puzzle 4 (page 41)

	Nouns	
Common	Proper	Collective
swan	China	gaggle
planet	Manchester	herd
apple	Barney	crowd

Verbs	Adjectives	Pronouns	Adverbs
argue	delicious	they	calmly
observe	expensive	she	carelessly
choose	miserable	ours	sadly

Puzzle 5 (page 42)

b	j	r	s	t	r	t	w
i	f	d	u	e	e	t	b
a	w	a	i	t	i	h	r
f	l	o	u	r	g	r	o
s	o	n	i	m	n	o	u
g	k	t	b	r	s	n	l
h	e	n	n	b	e	e	n
e	y	s	o	m	s	a	v

been   due
reign   wait
key   throne
flour

EXPANDED ANSWERS

NOTES

Answer these questions about the poem.

1 What is this poem about?

   _____

2 List three things the poet notices as he goes into the leisure centre.

   _____

   _____

3 Find a word in the poem rhyming with 'chute'.

   _____

4 What are the children in the café thinking?

   _____

5 Why is it hard to get dressed?

   _____

6 What does the line 'eyes are slowly closing' (line 39) describe?

   _____

7 List three things mentioned in the poem that children might not enjoy while at the leisure centre.

   _____

   _____

8 Why is the poem titled 'Leisure Centre, Pleasure Centre'?

   _____

   _____

   _____

23

Total

TEST 14: **Mixed**

Test time: 0 — 5 — 10 minutes

> Draw a line to match the words in each column that have the same letter string and pronunciation.

1   thorough   bough

2   rough   dough

3   nought   borough

4   though   thought

5   plough   tough

> Write a *definition* for each of these words.

6   dictionary
_____

7   diary
_____

8   ordinary
_____

9   February
_____

10 boundary
_____

24

Underline the *conjunctions* in each sentence.

11 At last Dad arrived home <u>so</u> we could eat our tea.

12 The wind rustled in the trees <u>as</u> darkness fell.

13 Jemma concentrated hard on her game of chess <u>because</u> it was an important match.

14 Daxa picked up the bags <u>and</u> carried them into the house.

15 The phone rang <u>but</u> nobody was home.

Add the missing commas to these sentences.

16 Lia packed her hairbrush, nightie and toothbrush.

17 Despite the tent being hot and stuffy, Abi found it fairly comfortable.

18–19 When Daniel returned from school, he did his homework, practised the piano, walked the dog and cleaned the fish tank.

20 Sarah ran down the lane, her school bag bumping against her leg.

TEST 15: **Vocabulary**

Test time: 0 ... 5 ... 10 minutes

Write an *antonym* for each word.

1   start   _____

2   push   _____

3   happy   _____

4   reward   _____

5   flexible   _____

Write these words in *alphabetical order*.

tartan   tarantula   tarnish   target   tart

6   (1) _____

7   (2) _____

8   (3) _____

9   (4) _____

10   (5) _____

Write the *diminutive* for each of these animals.

11   duck   _____

12   pig   _____

13   goose   _____

26

Write two sentences for this *homonym*. In each sentence the *homonym* must have a different meaning.

14–15 mine

(1) _____

_____

_____

(2) _____

_____

_____

The words used to describe something can change over time. Draw a line to match the words in each column that mean the same.

	Words used today	**Words used in the past**
16	dress	pitcher
17	glasses	satchel
18	schoolbag	wireless
19	radio	spectacles
20	jug	frock

Test 16: **Mixed**

Test time: 0 5 10 minutes

Change each of these *plural* words into its *singular* form.

1 engines _____

2 foxes _____

3 flies _____

4 scarves _____

5 drums _____

Add an *adjectival phrase* to complete each sentence.

6 The _____ car stopped quickly as the children began to cross the road.

7 Jess's camping party was great fun but we all got very wet in the _____ rain.

8 The _____ lambs raced across the field.

9 Callum always enjoyed picking the _____ _____ blackberries.

28

Add sure or ture to each of these to make a word.

10 expo_____

11 ma_____

12 signa_____

13 displea_____

14 minia_____

15 pres_____

Add the missing apostrophes.

16 Kates homework

17 my countrys flag

18 Liams computer

19 Meenas cakes

20 the birds nests

Time for a break! Go to Puzzle Page 41

Test 17: Grammar

Test time: 0 – 5 – 10 minutes

Underline the *adverbs* in these sentences.

1. The machinery clunked noisily before grinding to a stop.
2. The old lady walked awkwardly on the icy path.
3. Tess dressed sleepily after her alarm woke her.
4. Sanjay hastily ate his tea so he could join his friends.

Write three sentences, each of which includes an *adjective* and a *pronoun*.

5–6 _____

7–8 _____

9–10 _____

Write a more powerful *verb* for each of these *verbs*.

Example: look   *stare*

11   drink   _____

12   catch   _____

13   smell   _____

14   speak   _____

Sort these *nouns* into the correct columns in the table.

15–20 Wednesday   batch   kite

mosquito   Buckingham Palace   bunch

Common nouns	Proper nouns	Collective nouns
kite	Wednesday	batch
mosquito	Buckingham Palace	bunch

TEST 18: **Comprehension**

Test time: 0 – 5 – 10 minutes

Read this information carefully.

Great Balls of Gas *by Robin Kerrod*

1 Stars look like tiny bright specks in the night sky. But they are not tiny at all. They are in fact huge balls of searing hot gas. Stars look small only because they lie many
5 million, million kilometres away. If you could get close to a star, you would find that it looked like our Sun, because the Sun is a star too.

How big are stars?

10 We can measure the size of one star directly because it is so close. This is our own star, the Sun. The Sun measures nearly 1,400,000 kilometres across. Astronomers can work out the size of other stars too.
15 They have discovered that there are many stars smaller than the Sun, and also many much larger. Astronomers call the Sun a dwarf star. They know of red giant stars tens of times bigger.

20 ### Why do stars twinkle?

When we look up at the heavens, we can see thousands of stars shining down, but they do not give out a steady light. They seem to twinkle, or change
25 brightness all the time. In fact they do shine steadily but air currents in the Earth's atmosphere make the starlight bend this way and that. Some of the light gets into our eyes and some is bent away.
30 So, to us on Earth, the stars seem to twinkle.

Do stars last forever?

Just like living things, stars are born, grow older and, in time, die. After shining
35 steadily for some time the stars swell up into a red giant. Some red giants shrink into a white, then a black, dwarf. This will happen to the Sun one day. Other stars swell up from a red giant to a supergiant
40 before exploding as a supernova.

Answer these questions about the extract.

1 What are stars?

   _____

2 Why do stars look so small?

   _____

3 Which star is the easiest to measure?

   _____

4 What type of star do astronomers call the Sun?

   _____

5–6 In your own words describe why stars twinkle.

   _____

   _____

   _____

7 When referring to stars, what is a 'red giant'?

   _____

   _____

8 The information on stars asks and answers three questions. Write two more questions relating to stars that you would like to know the answers to.

   (1) _____

   _____

   (2) _____

   _____

Test 19: Mixed

Underline the words that are spoken.

1 "Where is your hat?" called Dad.

2 Angus screamed, "Watch out!"

3 "Let's go to the beach," suggested Maria.

4 "I can't wait until my birthday," said Joe.

Put a tick next to the words spelt correctly and a cross next to those spelt incorrectly.

5 suprise ☐

6 thought ☐

7 difficult ☐

8 exercise ☐

9 imagin ☐

10 accidentaly ☐

Underline the correct form of the *verb* to complete each sentence.

11 I did/done my homework quickly.

12 We was/were late for the party.

13 We did/done an excellent presentation.

14 I was/were tired after swimming.

Underline the *root word* in each of these words.

15 endless

16 printer

17 bicycle

18 trickery

19 collector

20 unclean

Test 20: Sentences

Test time: 0 5 10 minutes

Copy these sentences, adding the missing commas.

1 Riding on the tractor Kyle felt like a farmer just like his uncle.

2 The puppies chewed shoes furniture and their beds!

3 The ponies jumped the fence cantering up the lane towards the busy road.

4 Meena's sandwiches were filled with cheese ham and mayonnaise.

Write these words as a single word with a *contraction*.

Example: they have   *they've*

5 can not   _____

6 could have   _____

7 I will   _____

8 is not   _____

9 have not   _____

Copy this passage, adding the missing capital letters.

10–17 chris rushed out of the front door and headed down thresher lane. he was late for football again. ken, the coach, had threatened to throw him off the team if he didn't show for practice. why was it that his mum, liz, always arrived home late on a tuesday?

_____

_____

_____

_____

_____

_____

_____

_____

Write three sentences, each with a *fronted adverbial*.

18 _____

_____

19 _____

_____

20 _____

_____

Time for a break! Go to Puzzle Page 42

Puzzle 1

Add a letter to each empty space to find the answer.
Each word contains the letters OUGH.

The clues will help!

Clue						
A container from which animals eat or drink	___	___	O	U	G	H
A number	___	O	U	G	H	___
A mixture of flour and water	___	O	U	G	H	
Looked for	___	O	U	G	H	___
To dig over	___	___	O	U	G	H
A short, loud noise from your throat	___	O	U	G	H	
A serious shortage of water	___	___	O	U	G	H	___
An idea or opinion in your mind	___	___	O	U	G	H	___

Puzzle 2

Pair up a group of letters from each column to make a six-letter word.

nar	narrow	nal
sig	_____	ugh
lov	_____	cle
tho	_____	son
cir	_____	rge
sch	_____	row
fri	_____	ief
les	_____	ely
cha	_____	dow
bel	_____	ght
win	_____	ool

Puzzle 3

With a line, match the *definition* with the correct word.

(tricycle)

(duet)

(decade)

(double)

(century) (triplets)

(quartet) (duel)

a song sung by two people

a three-wheeled bike

three babies born at a similar
time to the same mother

a fight between two people

a group of four musicians

a hundred years

two of the same thing

a ten-year period

Puzzle 4

Look carefully at these words. Put them in the correct place in the table.

China swan sadly argue ours carelessly gaggle delicious she miserable observe expensive calmly herd Barney planet apple Manchester crowd they choose

| Nouns |||
Common	Proper	Collective

Verbs	Adjectives	Pronouns	Adverbs

Puzzle 5

Try this homophone hunt.

b	j	r	s	t	r	t	w
i	f	d	u	e	e	t	b
a	w	a	i	t	i	h	r
f	l	o	u	r	g	r	o
s	o	n	i	m	n	o	u
g	k	t	b	t	s	n	l
h	e	n	n	b	e	e	n
e	y	s	o	m	s	a	v

Find a *homophone* in the wordsearch for each of the following words. Write the words you have found.

bean　　　＿＿＿＿＿＿＿＿＿＿

rain　　　＿＿＿＿＿＿＿＿＿＿

quay　　　＿＿＿＿＿＿＿＿＿＿

flower　　＿＿＿＿＿＿＿＿＿＿

dew　　　＿＿＿＿＿＿＿＿＿＿

weight　　＿＿＿＿＿＿＿＿＿＿

thrown　　＿＿＿＿＿＿＿＿＿＿

Key words

Some special words are used in this book. You will find them picked out in *italics*. These words are explained here.

adjectival phrase	a group of words describing a noun
adjective	a word that describes somebody or something
adverb	a word that gives extra meaning to a verb
adverbial phrase	a word or phrase that makes the meaning of a verb, adjective or another adverb more specific, for example, The Cheshire cat vanished quite slowly, beginning with the end of its tail.
alphabetical order	words arranged in the order of the letters in the alphabet
antonym	a word with a meaning opposite to another word, for example, hot/cold
collective noun	a word referring to a group of things, for example, a *swarm* of bees
common noun	a noun referring to a person, place or thing, for example, teacher, castle, book; it does not start with a capital letter
compound word	a word made up of two other words, for example, football
conjunction	a word used to link sentences, phrases or words, for example, and, but
contraction	two words shortened into one with an apostrophe placed where the letter/s have been dropped, for example, do not/don't
definition	the meaning of a word
diminutive	a word implying smallness, for example, duckling
fronted adverbial	an adverbial that has been moved before the verb, for example, The day after tomorrow, I'm going on holiday.
homonym	a word that has the same spelling or sound as another word but a different meaning, for example, turn *left*, we *left* the room
homophone	a word that has the same sound as another but a different meaning or spelling, for example, right/write
noun	a naming word for a person, place, feeling or thing
noun phrase	a group of words containing a noun and other words that describe the noun, for example, the small black cat
phrase	a group of words that act as a unit
plural	more than one, for example, cats
prefix	a group of letters added to the beginning of a word, for example, un, dis
pronoun	a word that can be used instead of a noun, for example, his
proper noun	the specific name or title of a person or a place, for example, Ben, London
root word	a word to which a prefix or suffix can be added to make another word, for example, quick – *quick*ly
singular	one of something, for example, cat
suffix	a group of letters added to the end of a word, for example, ly, ful
synonym	a word with a very similar meaning to another word, for example, quick/fast
verb	a 'doing' or 'being' word

Progress Grid

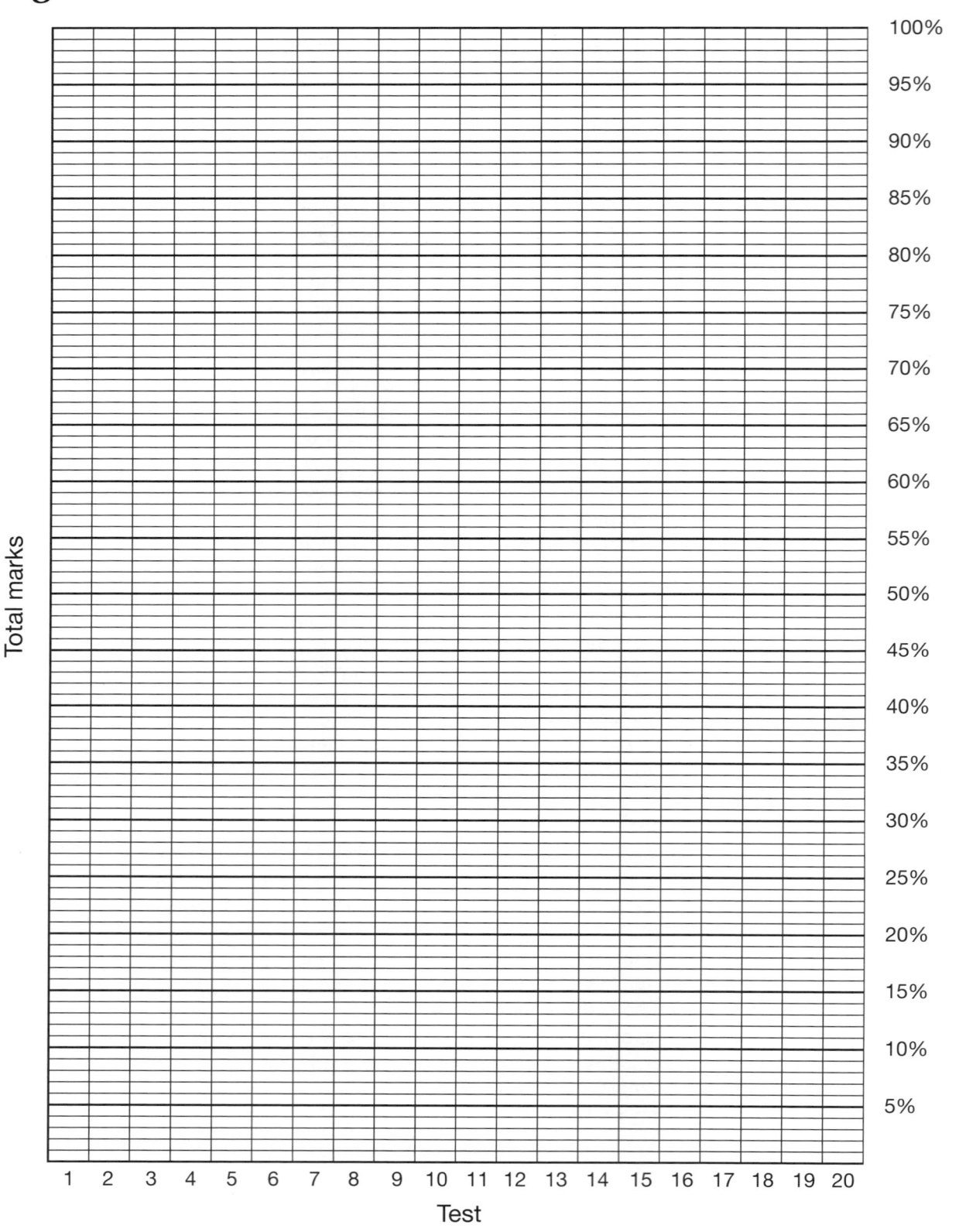